HISTORY & GEOGRA
HISTORY AND GEO
OF OUR STATE

MW01121649

CONTENTS

Author: **Alpha Omega Staff**

Editor: Alan Christopherson, M.S.

Graphic Design: Alpha Omega Staff

Alpha Omega Publications®

804 N. 2nd Ave. E., Rock Rapids, IA 51246-1759

HISTORY AND GEOGRAPHY OF OUR STATES

The states in our country have grown through a series of historical events that have helped make each state unique. These events include the exploration, settlement, agricultural and industrial developments, and urbanization of an area. These events are also directly related to the geography of that area.

In this LIFEPAC® you will study the geography of four regions in the United States. You will learn about **landforms**, climate, natural resources, agriculture, industry, living patterns, and important historical events in each of these regions. By studying the elements in the environment, you will learn how these things have shaped our national history and culture. This knowledge helps you to understand the world you live in today and helps you to plan for the world you will live in tomorrow.

OBJECTIVES

Read these objectives. The objectives tell you what you will be able to do when you have successfully completed this LIFEPAC.

When you have finished this LIFEPAC, you should be able to:

1. Use maps and globes as a source of information about the United States.

2. Describe the landforms, climate, and early history of the United States.

3. Describe the landforms and climate in your own state.

4. Explain the effect of climate and landforms on occupations, agriculture, and industry in your own state and in the four regions of the United States.

Survey the LIFEPAC. Ask yourself some questions about this study. Write your questions here

_____

_____

_____

_____

_____

_____

_____

_____

_____

_____

_____

I. LOOKING AT THE UNITED STATES

Geography, the study of God's earth and how people adapt to conditions on earth, can help you to understand history. The knowledge and skills of geography provide the background, the scenery, for a better view of historical events.

In this section of the LIFEPAC, you will learn about the location of the United States in the world. You will also learn about rivers, harbors, mountains, **plateaus**, climate, and natural resources. You will study the early history and exploration of the United States. You will use this information to describe the geography and historical events that are important in your own state.

SECTION OBJECTIVES

Review these objectives. When you have completed this section, you should be able to:

1. Use maps and globes as a source of information about the United States.

2. Describe the landforms, climate, and early history of the United States.

3. Describe the landforms and climate in your own state.

VOCABULARY

Study these words to enhance your learning success in this section.

archaeologist (är kē- ol´ u jist). A person who studies ancient cultures.

basin (bā´ sun). An area of land that is surrounded by higher land and may be drained by a river.

canyon (kan´ yun). A deep narrow valley with steep sides.

contiguous (kun tig´ yu̇ us). Touching; joining.

continent (kon´ tu nunt). One of the largest bodies of land on earth.

Continental Divide (kon tu nen´ tul du vīd´). A line that separates the flow of rivers to the opposite sides of the continent.

cultivation (kul tu vā´ shun). The process by which the soil is prepared and used to grow crops.

delta (del´ tu). The land deposited at the mouth of the river.

elevation (el u vā´ shun). Distance above sea level.

glacier (glā´ shur). A large mass of slowly moving ice.

gorge (gôrj). A narrow passage.

landform (land´ fôrm). A natural feature of the earth.

natural region (nach´ ur ul rē´ jun). An area formed by natural landforms.

peninsula (pu nin´ su lu). A piece of land almost surrounded by water.

plateau (pla tō). A large level area of elevated land.

political region (pu lit´ u kul rē´ jun). An area defined by people; state, city, country, and so forth.

Note: All vocabulary words in this LIFEPAC appear in **boldface** print the first time they are used. If you are not sure of the meaning when you are reading, study the definitions given.

Pronunciation Key: hat, āge, cãre, fär; let, ēqual, tėrm; it, īce; hot, ōpen, ôrder; oil; out; cup, pùt, rüle; child; long; thin; /TH/ for then; /zh/ for measure; /u/ represents /a/ in about, /e/ in taken, /i/ in pencil, /o/ in lemon, and /u/ in circus.

GEOGRAPHY OF THE UNITED STATES

The study of geography includes the physical features and the location of countries and regions on the earth's surface. Life in any area of the world is affected by where that area is located and by its physical features.

The earth has several large land masses called **continents**. North America is one such land mass, and the United States is just one country on that continent. To understand the United States better, you must understand its location on the earth and its geographical features. Life in the United States is influenced by climate, size, and **landforms**.

Geographical location. God created the continents and oceans of our world. Arctic, Atlantic, Indian, and Pacific are the names of the four oceans on our earth. These oceans—along with the smaller seas, bays, gulfs, lakes, and rivers—cover almost three-fourths of the earth's surface.

When you look at the map or globe you will see six large land masses. Geographers say we have seven continents. One land mass is so large that it is divided into two continents, Europe and Asia. The other continents are Africa, Antarctica, Australia, South America, and North America.

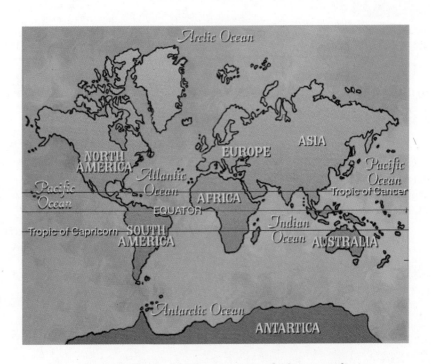

Continents and oceans of the earth

3

The United States is on the continent of North America. The continent also includes Canada to the north, Mexico and Central America to the south, the Caribbean Islands to the southeast, and the island of Greenland to the northeast.

Our nation has fifty states. Forty-eight of these states are connected to each other. They are called the continental or **contiguous** states. Two of the fifty states, Alaska and Hawaii, are separated from the others. Alaska is north of the contiguous states on the North American continent. Hawaii is a series of islands in the Pacific Ocean west of the continental states.

The continental United States has four different time zones: Eastern, Central, Mountain, and Pacific.

The United States is about halfway between the North Pole and the equator. The United States is in the Northern Hemisphere, which is the more populated of the two hemispheres.

The Pacific Ocean is on the western side of the nation, and the Atlantic is on the east. These oceans have been both trade routes for American goods and barriers which have kept foreign wars from American soil.

The United States is a large country with space for farming, industry, cities, recreation, and many people.

The United States has developed from a land of sparsely-populated tribal groups to the most powerful nation on earth in the span of 300 years.

Time Zones

Pacific Standard Time 2 P.M.	Mountain Standard Time 3 P.M.	Central Standard Time 4 P.M.	Eastern Standard Time 5 P.M.

Match the following vocabulary words with their definitions.

1.1 _____ archaeologist

1.2 _____ basin

1.3 _____ canyon

1.4 _____ contiguous

1.5 _____ continent

1.6 _____ Continental Divide

1.7 _____ cultivation

1.8 _____ delta

a. the land deposited at the mouth of the river.

b. a person who studies ancient cultures.

c. the process by which the soil is prepared and used to grow crops.

d. an area of land that is surrounded by higher land and may be drained by a river.

e. a line that separates the flow of rivers to the opposite sides of the continent.

f. a deep narrow valley with steep sides.

g. one of the largest bodies of land on earth.

h. touching; joining.

4

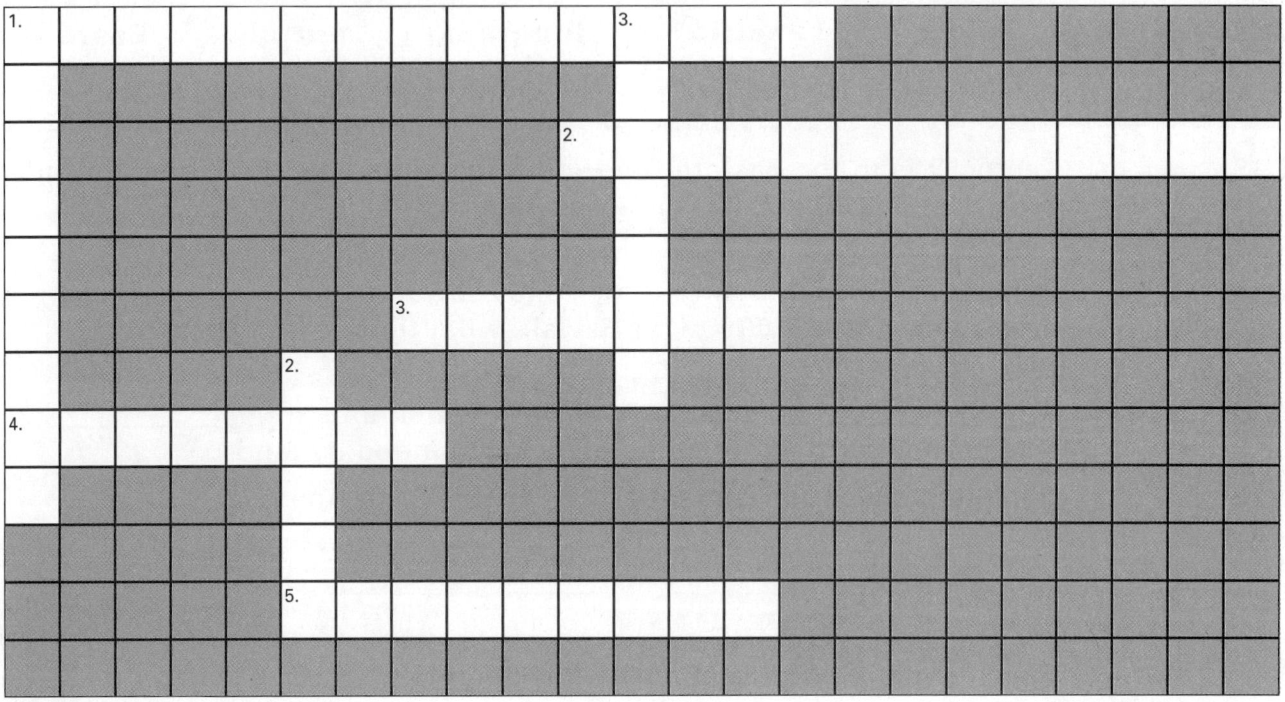

[Crossword grid]

Complete the vocabulary crossword.

1.9

ACROSS

1. An area defined by people; state, city, country, and so forth.
2. An area formed by natural landforms.
3. A large level area of elevated land.
4. A natural feature of the earth.
5. Distance above sea level.

DOWN

1. A piece of land almost surrounded by water.
2. A narrow passage.
3. A large mass of slowly moving ice.

Complete these statements.

1.10 Referring to the first map, name two continents through which the equator goes.

a. _____ b. _____

1.11 The Tropic of _____ passes through Australia and Africa.

1.12 The Tropic of _____ passes through North America, Africa, and Asia.

Alaska-Hawaii	Yukon	Pacific	Mountain	Central	Eastern
9:30 A.M.	10:30 A.M.	11:30 A.M.	12:30 P.M.	1:30 P.M.	2:30 P.M.

1.13   Kentucky is in the Eastern time zone. Montana is in the Mountain time zone. If it is 2:30 P.M. in Kentucky, what time is it in Montana?

_____

1.14   Oklahoma is in the Central time zone. Hawaii is in the Alaska-Hawaii time zone. If it is 2:00 A.M. in Hawaii, what time is it in Oklahoma?

_____

1.15   A(n) _____ is a large body of water, and a(n) _____ is smaller and partially or completely surrounded by land.

1.16   Name the six countries that are a part of North America.

    a. _____   d. _____

    b. _____   e. _____

    c. _____   f. _____

1.17   Which state is northwest of the forty-eight contiguous states?

_____

1.18   The state that is a chain of islands not a part of the continent of North America is _____ .

Highlands, lowlands, and plains. The natural landform regions in the United States are thousands of years old. **Natural regions** are different from **political regions**. A state, a country, and a city are political regions. People have divided the land and named these regions.

A natural region is God-given. Forests, mountains, rivers, **plateaus**, swamps, lakes, **glaciers**, and plains are examples of natural regions.

The following map shows the location of the natural landform regions in the United States.

Landform Regions of the United States

6

The Appalachian Highlands are the oldest mountain system in the United States. The mountains are not very high, but in many places they are very rugged. Major mountain ranges in this system are the Adirondack Mountains, Allegheny Mountains, Black Mountains, Blue Ridge Mountains, Catskill Mountains, Green Mountains, Great Smokey Mountains, and the White Mountains. The highest peak in the Eastern U.S. is Mount Mitchell, which rises 6,684 feet above sea level, in the Black Mountains near Asheville, North Carolina.

These mountains form ridges that run from northeast to southwest and are separated by narrow valleys. The mountains also divide the river flow. On the east, rivers flow toward the east and over the coastal plain. On the other side the rivers flow westward and toward the Central Lowlands.

The Appalachian Plateau was flat at one time, but has been worn down over the centuries by rivers and streams. It is now almost as rugged as the surrounding highlands.

The Piedmont Plateau is a hard, rocky surface between the highlands and the coastal plain. At the edge of this plateau are many waterfalls. Through the years, the rivers that flow down the hills of the Appalachian Highlands and across the flat rocky plateau have gouged deep valleys in the sandy soil of the coastal plain and have formed waterfalls.

▶▶▶ Complete these statements.

1.19   The oldest mountain system in the United States is the
        _____ Highlands.

1.20   Name seven mountain ranges that are part of the Appalachian Highlands.

   a. _____   e. _____

   b. _____   f. _____

   c. _____   g. _____

   d. _____

1.21   The hard, rocky surface between the Appalachian Highlands and the coastal plains is called the _____ Plateau.

1.22   Complete the names of the western natural landform regions of the continental states:

   a. _____   Mountains and Valleys

   b. _____   Region

   c. _____   Mountain Region

1.23   Complete the names of the central and eastern natural landform regions of the continental states:

   a. _____ and b. _____ Coastal Plains

   c. _____ Lowlands and d. _____ Plains

   e. _____ Uplands

   f. _____ Highlands

   g. _____ Highlands

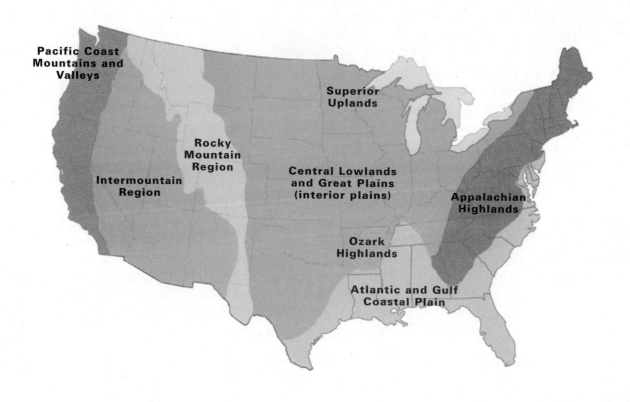

The Atlantic and Gulf coastal plains are level and made of layers of sand and clay. These plains are close to sea level. The land is generally flat and easily **cultivated** because of the loose, sandy soil. Rivers that flow across this plain deposit clay, sand, gravel, and silt eroded from the highlands. A large deposit of these materials at the mouth of a river is called a river **delta**. The Mississippi has a large delta region reaching out into the Gulf of Mexico.

Some rivers have cut deeper valleys into the coastal plain, and in some places the ocean has flowed inland across the river valley to form a large bay. When the ocean covers a river valley and the nearby land, geographers call the bay a drowned river valley. Chesapeake Bay, Delaware Bay, Mobile Bay, and New York Bay are all drowned river valleys. The Everglades swampland and slow-moving streams called bayous are features of the southern coastal plain.

The Ozark Highlands are a small range of low mountains and hills. The Ozark Plateau, the Boston Mountains, and the Ouachita Mountains are part of this highland region found in the South Central area of our country.

The Central Lowlands extend from the Appalachians to the Great Plains. The soil and climate of the Central Lowlands produces dense forests. The climate of the Great Plains, however, supports only a few trees and many miles of rich grassland.

The Central Lowlands slope gently to the west, and the Plains slope toward the east. The rivers in this region are part of the Mississippi River Basin.

The Mississippi River, the largest river in our country, begins at Lake Itasca in Northern Minnesota. The Missouri River, the Ohio River, the Tennessee River, and a number of smaller rivers flow into the Mississippi. These rivers are tributaries of the Mississippi River. In the northwest part of this region are two highland areas, the Badlands and the Black Hills.

Complete these activities.

1.24 Name the rivers of the Central Lowlands and Great Plains.

a. _____ c. _____

b. _____ d. _____

1.25 The Central Lowlands lie between the _____
Highlands and the _____ Plains.

1.26 Select the region where the following landform is found:
Green Mountains
a. Appalachian Highlands
b. Coastal Plains
c. Great Plains

1.27 Select the region where the following landform is found:
Badlands
a. Appalachian Highlands
b. Coastal Plains
c. Great Plains

1.28 Select the region where the following landform is found:
Bayous
a. Appalachian Highlands
b. Coastal Plains
c. Great Plains

1.29 Select the region where the following landform is found:
Piedmont Plateau
a. Appalachian Highlands
b. Coastal Plains
c. Great Plains

1.30 Select the region where the following landform is found:
Delaware Bay
a. Appalachian Highlands
b. Coastal Plains
c. Great Plains

1.31 Select the region where the following landform is found:
Mount Mitchell
a. Appalachian Highlands
b. Coastal Plains
c. Great Plains

1.32 Select the region where the following landform is found:
Everglades
a. Appalachian Highlands
b. Coastal Plains
c. Great Plains

1.33 Select the region where the following landform is found:
Black Hills
a. Appalachian Highlands
b. Coastal Plains
c. Great Plains

The Superior Uplands have low mountains and rolling hills. The land is heavily wooded. Many lakes dot the land and in some places the soil is often too wet for farming.

The mountain regions. The Rocky Mountains are high, rugged mountains with sharp, rocky peaks. Geologists call these mountains "young mountains." The Laramie Plain, a great plateau, divides the Rockies into two parts, the Southern Rockies are the highest mountains of the system. Fourteen of the peaks in the Rockies rise higher than fourteen thousand feet above sea level and snow is on the ground all year at the higher **elevations**.

The **Continental Divide** is located in these mountains. All of the rain that falls on our continent either collects in streams, rivers, and lakes, or it evaporates. The streams and rivers that flow on the eastern side of the Continental Divide will eventually reach the Atlantic Ocean. The water that flows down the western side of the Continental Divide will eventually reach the Pacific Ocean.

The Intermountain region is located between the Rocky Mountains and the mountains and valleys of the Pacific Coast. This region has many **basins** and plateaus.

The plateaus are not as high as the nearby mountains but are much higher in elevation than the eastern part of our country. Rivers have cut deep valleys into these plateaus. Such steep-sided valleys are called **canyons** and **gorges**. One part of this region is called the Great Basin. A basin is bowl-shaped land. Rain that falls in the Great Basin does not collect in rivers that reach the ocean. Instead the rain sinks into the dry earth or gathers in salt lakes or rivers that evaporate.

The Sierra Nevadas, the Cascades, and the Coast Ranges are the mountains in the Pacific Coast region. The inland ranges are steep and rugged with the highest peaks snow-covered all year. Mount Whitney in the Sierra Nevada Range is the highest peak in the continental United States.

The inland and coastal ranges surround and protect a large central valley in the south and a strip of fertile lowland in the north extending from the Willamette River valley to the Puget Sound area.

Alaska is part of the Pacific Coast region. Hawaii consists of several islands that are the tops of large volcanoes extending above sea level from the floor of the Pacific Ocean.

▶ ▶ ▶ **Complete this activity.**

1.34   Name the three mountain ranges in the Pacific coast region.

a._____   b._____   c._____

Match these items.

1.35 _____ basin

1.36 _____ canyon

1.37 _____ Continental Divide

1.38 _____ young mountains

1.39 _____ tops of volcanoes

a. a line that separates the flow of rivers to the opposite sides of the continent

b. Hawaiian islands

c. bowl-shaped land

d. high and rugged with sharp, rocky peaks

e. a deep, narrow valley with steep sides

EARLY HISTORY OF THE UNITED STATES

Hundreds of years before the first Europeans found their way to the new world, people lived on the land we call the United States. Columbus named these people Indians because he believed he had landed near India. Today the descendants of these people call themselves Native Americans.

Many historians believe that the Native Americans came to this land from Asia and settled in different parts of North and South America. **Archaeologists** tell us that these people were building mounds in the central part of our country during the time Christ was walking the dusty roads of Jerusalem.

Geography played an important role in the lives of these people. Those who lived in the dense forests made houses of wood and hunted or fished for their food. Those who lived on fertile soil grew their own food. Others who lived on the prairie or in the desert made their houses of grass or carved their homes in the cliff sides. Many tribes of Native Americans lived in North America. Their cultures and languages were all different. Intertribal warfare was common.

Explorers. Many historians believe the earliest European explorers of the North American continent were the Vikings of Norway. They sailed in long ships to Iceland, then to Greenland, and finally to Newfoundland, off the coast of eastern Canada, where they established a settlement about the year A.D. 1000.

The Spanish explorers, beginning with Christopher Columbus, landed on a small island southeast of Florida in 1492. The king and queen of Spain had financed the journey, so Columbus claimed the land for Spain. Columbus made four trips to the New World searching for a route to the Indies and their treasures.

Ponce de León, one of the explorers that followed Columbus to the New World, sailed from the island of Hispaniola (present day Santo Domingo) and landed on the Florida **peninsula** in 1513. He was looking for gold in the New World, as were most of the explorers. He explored the coast and named the land.

An English explorer, John Cabot, was determined that England should share in any riches that the New World had to offer. He believed that Columbus had found a route to the Spice Islands and that he would be able to locate a shorter route. He persuaded England to help him cross the Atlantic. Cabot claimed Newfoundland, which he named, and the eastern seacoast for England. He sailed down the coast to the present-day Carolinas.

The French explorer Jacques Cartier sailed across the Atlantic to the Gulf of St. Lawrence off the western tip of Newfoundland, and far up the St. Lawrence River in 1534–35.

In 1608 Samuel de Champlain started a French colony on the banks of the St. Lawrence River at Quebec. He then sailed farther inland and discovered the Great Lakes. Jacques Marquette and Louis Jolliet followed Champlain and discovered the northern Mississippi River. They sailed south on the "mighty river." However, French explorer Robert de La Salle was the one who explored the Mississippi all the way to the Gulf of Mexico and claimed all the land for France in 1682.

A Dutch explorer, Henry Hudson, found an opening on the eastern coast of America that he thought might be a route to the Pacific Ocean. He sailed inland past the isle of Manhattan which was claimed by the Dutch. Soon Hudson discovered that the river would not lead him into the Pacific. The next time Hudson returned to America, he was hired by the English, and he discovered a great bay which he claimed for the English. The Hudson River and Hudson Bay were both named in his honor.

The early explorers were looking for a route through the Northern American continent to reach the riches of China. The first explorer to finally sail a ship through Canada's icy Northwest Passage to the Pacific Ocean was the Norwegian, Roald Amudsen. That did not happen until 1906. However, the search for the route was a major impetus behind the exploration of the new world.

In 1539 Hernando de Soto explored inland Florida and traveled northwest until he and his men were stopped by a river the Indians called "Father of Water," the Mississippi. The men crossed the river but soon turned back and sailed south toward the mouth of the Mississippi claiming this land for Spain.

Coronado, another Spaniard, traveled to Mexico where the Spanish had found tremendous amounts of gold. He left Mexico with a troop of soldiers and African slaves in 1540 to look for more gold. These hardy men traveled over the Southwest region of the country that was later to be called the United States. They left records of their discovery of the Grand Canyon and the land in Arizona and New Mexico.

Captain Vitus Bering of the Russian navy landed on Alaska in 1741. Many Russian explorers followed to chart the lands of Alaska and the northwest coastline.

Answer *true* **or** *false.*

1.40 _____ Native Americans had migrated into central North America by the time of Christ.

1.41 _____ All tribes of native Americans were alike.

1.42 _____ Columbus called these people Indians.

1.43 _____ Some Indians built their homes on cliff sides.

Write the correct answer on each line.

1.44 Christopher Columbus claimed the New World for_____.
   a. England   b. France   c. Spain

1.45 Columbus sailed to the New World _____times.
   a   two   b. four   c. eight

1.46 The man who did not explore Florida was _____.
   a. Ponce de León   b. Coronado   c. Hernando de Soto

1.47 Samuel de Champlain sailed up the _____ and established a colony at Quebec.
   a. Hudson River   b. Mohawk River   c. St. Lawrence River

1.48 The man who sailed from Newfoundland down the eastern coast to the present-day Carolinas and claimed this land for England was

   _____.

   a. Hudson   b. Cabot   c. Cartier

1.49   The man who sailed down the Mississippi River from the Great Lakes to the Gulf of Mexico and claimed this land for France was _____

        a. Cartier   b. La Salle   c. Ponce de León

1.50   The Grand Canyon was discovered by _____ .

        a. Coronado   b. Marquette   c. De Soto

Settlement. The settlement of the United States varied greatly from state to state. The experiences of the Pilgrims in Massachusetts were different from the experiences of the pioneers that moved into Kansas on the eve of the Civil War and different from those who sailed around Cape Horn or those who rode in wagon trains across the Oregon Trail to reach the far West.

The first state was admitted to the Union in 1787; the last states, in 1959. During the 172 years between the admissions of the first state and the last one, forty-eight other states were admitted. The United States expanded from ocean to ocean, adding a northern "giant" and a Pacific "jewel."

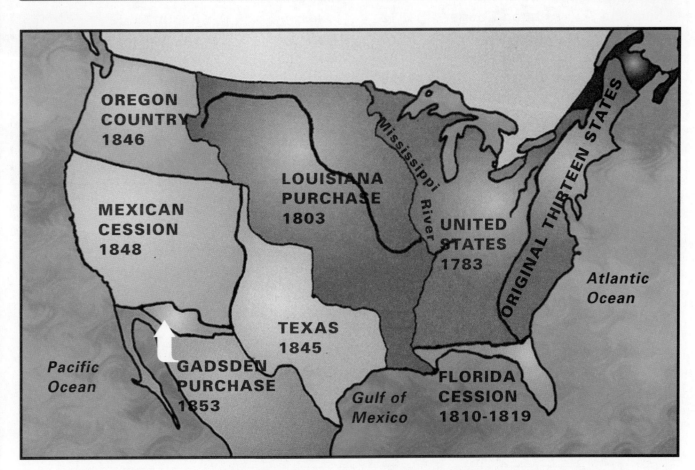

This map of the United States in 1853 helps to show its rapid growth.

13

THE UNITED STATES OF AMERICA

State	Capital City	Year Admitted	State	Capital City	Year Admitted
Alabama	Montgomery	1819	Montana	Helena	1889
Alaska	Juneau	1959	Nebraska	Lincoln	1867
Arizona	Phoenix	1912	Nevada	Carson City	1864
Arkansas	Little Rock	1836	New Hampshire	Concord	1788
California	Sacramento	1850	New Jersey	Trenton	1787
Colorado	Denver	1876	New Mexico	Santa Fe	1912
Connecticut	Hartford	1788	New York	Albany	1788
Delaware	Dover	1787	North Carolina	Raleigh	1789
Florida	Tallahassee	1845	North Dakota	Bismarck	1889
Georgia	Atlanta	1788	Ohio	Columbus	1803
Hawaii	Honolulu	1959	Oklahoma	Oklahoma City	1907
Idaho	Boise	1890	Oregon	Salem	1859
Illinois	Springfield	1818	Pennsylvania	Harrisburg	1787
Indiana	Indianapolis	1816	Rhode Island	Providence	1790
Iowa	Des Moines	1846	South Carolina	Columbia	1788
Kansas	Topeka	1861	South Dakota	Pierre	1889
Kentucky	Frankfort	1792	Tennessee	Nashville	1796
Louisiana	Baton Rouge	1812	Texas	Austin	1845
Maine	Augusta	1820	Utah	Salt Lake City	1896
Maryland	Annapolis	1788	Vermont	Montpelier	1791
Massachusetts	Boston	1788	Virginia	Richmond	1788
Michigan	Lansing	1837	Washington	Olympia	1889
Minnesota	St. Paul	1858	West Virginia	Charleston	1863
Mississippi	Jackson	1817	Wisconsin	Madison	1848
Missouri	Jefferson	1821	Wyoming	Cheyenne	1890

Complete these activities.

1.51   Circle the original thirteen states which were "admitted" between 1787-1790.

1.52   How many states were admitted to the union in the second half of the 19th century? _____

1.53   Name the three states admitted to the Union after the original thirteen but before the end of the 18th century.

      a. _____

      b. _____

      c. _____

1.54   Name the five states admitted to the Union in the twentieth century.

      a. _____   b. _____   c. _____

      d. _____   e. _____

Review the material in this section in preparation for the Self Test. The Self Test will check your mastery of this particular section. The items missed on this Self Test will indicate specific areas where restudy is needed for mastery.

SELF TEST 1

Match these items (each answer, 2 points).

1.01	_____ political region	a. north-central U.S.A.; contains many lakes
1.02	_____ Cabot	b. drowned river valley
1.03	_____ plateau	c. state, city
1.04	_____ De Soto	d. level area of elevated land
1.05	_____ sea	e. named Newfoundland
1.06	_____ Chesapeake Bay	f. explored Arizona and New Mexico
1.07	_____ Superior Uplands	g. large body of water partly or wholly surrounded by land
1.08	_____ Coronado	h. explored Florida
1.09	_____ Rocky Mountains	i. divided by the Laramie Plain
1.010	_____ Appalachian Highland	j. includes Adirondacks, and Catskills

Write *true* **or** *false* (each answer, 1 point).

1.011 _____ Europe and Asia are on the same large land mass.

1.012 _____ Land covers more than one-half of the earth.

1.013 _____ The United States is the only country on the North American continent.

1.014 _____ One reason why the United States has grown to be large and prosperous is its climate.

1.015 _____ The Piedmont Plateau has soft, sandy soil.

1.016 _____ The Missouri River is the largest river in the United States.

1.017 _____ A peninsula is land that extends into the water and is almost surrounded by the water.

1.018 _____ The only part of the United States explored by Russia was the Northwest coastline.

1.019 _____ The land along the Mississippi was claimed for France by Ponce de León.

1.020 _____ The interior area that supported the fewest trees was the Great Plains.

Write the letter of the correct answer on the line (each answer, 2 points).

1.021 _____ The area around New York was claimed by the _____.
  a. Russians   b. Dutch   c. Germans

1.022 _____ Most of the Southern United States was explored by the _____.
  a. English   b. Spanish   c. French

1.023 _____ A natural region includes a _____.
  a. plateau   b. city   c. garden

15

1.024   The Pacific Coast Mountains_____.
           a. are worn down
           b. are the biggest range in the United States
           c. include the highest peak on the continental U.S.

1.025   The first explorers of the North American continent were_____.
           a. Spanish   b. Norwegian   c. French

1.026   Which of these states was admitted to the Union in the 20th century?
           a. Vermont
           b. Arizona
           c. California

Complete this statement (each answer, 3 points).

1.027   The seven continents are
           a. _____ ,
           b. _____ ,
           c. _____ ,
           d. _____ ,
           e. _____ ,
           f. _____ , and
           g. _____ .

50 / 63

Score _____
Teacher check _____
               Initial   Date

II. PHYSICAL AND CULTURAL REGIONS OF THE NORTHEAST AND THE SOUTH

In this LIFEPAC, the fifty states have been grouped into four regions. Each region has geographical, historical, and political significance. The regions you will study in this section are the Northeast and the South.

As you study the history and geography of each region you might ask yourself these questions:

1. How do the physical features of the land affect agriculture, industry, transportation, and living patterns?

2. What effect does the climate have on agriculture, industry, transportation, and living patterns?

3. What are the natural resources of the region, and how are they used?

4. How were the important historical events affected by the geography of the region?

SECTION OBJECTIVES

Review these objectives. When you have completed this section, you should be able to:

1. Use maps and globes as a source of information about the Northeastern and Southern United States.

2. Describe the landforms, climate, and early history of the Northeastern and Southern United States.

3. Describe the landforms and climate in your own state.

4. Explain the effect of climate and landforms on occupations, agriculture, and industry in your own state and in the four regions of the United States.

· ·

VOCABULARY

Study these words to enhance your learning success in this section.

deciduous (di sij´ u̇ us). Trees that lose their leaves in the fall.

fall line (fôl līn). The area where rivers fall from the Piedmont Plateau to the coastal plains.

fishing banks (fish´ ing bangks). A shallow place in the ocean where fish feed.

growing season (grō´ ing sē´ zun). The time between the last killing frost in the spring, and the first killing frost in the fall.

hurricane (hėr´ u kān). A whirling storm that forms over the ocean in tropical regions.

textile (teks´ tul). Cloth.

wood pulp (wu̇d pulp). Wood that is ground into a thick liquid and used to make paper and paper products.

· ·

NORTHEAST

The Northeast was one of the first areas of the United States to be explored by Europeans. The Vikings explored parts of this region almost one thousand years ago. Later, Cabot sailed along the eastern coast and claimed the area around New York for the Dutch, naming it New Holland.

The states in the Northeast region are Connecticut, Delaware, Maine, Maryland, Massachusetts, New Hampshire, New Jersey, New York, Pennsylvania, Rhode Island, and Vermont. Washington D.C., our nation's capital, is also considered a part of the Northeast. Connecticut, Maine, Rhode Island, New Hampshire, and Vermont are called the New England states.

Northeast States

New Hampshire
Maine
Vermont
New York
Massachusetts
Rhode Island
Connecticut
Pennsylvania
New Jersey
Delaware
Maryland
Washington D.C.

Geography of the Northeast. The natural landforms in the Northeast are the Atlantic Coastal Plain, the Appalachian Highlands, and other lowlands. There is evidence that glaciers once covered the northeastern United States. The glaciers moved southward carrying tons of rock and scraping away the soil in some places. They rounded the tops of mountains and dug holes into the rocky ground. When the glaciers retreated, the big holes retained water and became lakes. In New England the glaciers scoured the land and left the soil rough and rocky and thin.

The largest lakes in this area are Lake Champlain between Vermont and New York, Moosehead Lake in Maine, and Winnepesaukee Lake in New Hampshire. Two of the Great Lakes, Erie and Ontario, are also in this region.

Important rivers in the region are the Connecticut, Hudson, Mohawk, Susquehanna, and Paucatuck. The coastline in this region is rough and rocky and has many small bays and inlets. Three large bays are the Chesapeake Bay in Maryland, the Delaware Bay, and the New York Bay. Islands and peninsulas are also found along this coastline. Long Island in New York is one of the best known islands. Cape Cod in Massachusetts and Mount Desert Island in Maine are peninsulas.

Much of the land area in the Northeast is highlands. The mountain ranges include the Adirondack, the Allegheny, the Catskill, the Green, and the White mountain ranges. Between these ranges lie valleys where many farms are located. Other farms are on the inland plain area in western New York and northwestern Pennsylvania. The Erie-Ontario Lowland lies to the south of these two Great Lakes. The famous Niagara Falls is between the lakes.

Climate. The climate in the Northeast varies from place to place. The climate in any area is affected primarily by (1) the distance from the equator, (2) the distance from a large body of water, and (3) the altitude.

Through most of the Northeast the weather is cool in the fall. The cool weather triggers a reaction in the trees that makes the leaves of **deciduous** trees turn bright colors and fall to the ground. The Northeast is famous for the beauty of the trees in autumn. In the winter heavy snow falls in the highlands and on the interior plain. The weather is very cold and the snow may stay on the ground all winter. People come to the mountains to ski and snowmobile.

In other parts of the Northeast the winters are not so severe. On the coastal plain the weather is milder. Large bodies of water do not lose heat as rapidly as the land.

In the winter the temperature of the Atlantic Ocean is warmer than the temperature of the land. The coastland is also warmed by the wind that blows across the Atlantic.

Spring comes to the southern part of the Northeast first. Around Washington D.C. the trees begin to blossom in April. Spring is the beginning of the growing season for farmers. The **growing season** starts after the last killing frost and it is not over until the first killing frost of the winter. Around Washington D.C. the growing season is six to seven months long. In some places in the highlands and in Maine the growing season is less than three months long.

Natural resources. Wood pulp (for paper and cardboard) and Christmas trees are important products of Northeastern forests. Clay, sand, gravel, limestone, granite, marble, zinc, iron ore, and coal are mined in the Northeast. The coast has an important fishing industry. Clams, lobsters, and oysters are abundant. Further out on the **fishing banks**, fishermen catch whiting, ocean perch, flounder, scallops, cod, haddock, and menhaden (a kind of herring).

• •

 **Match these vocabulary words with their definitions.**

2.1 _____ deciduous

2.2 _____ fall line

2.3 _____ fishing banks

2.4 _____ growing season

2.5 _____ hurricane

2.6 _____ textile

2.7 _____ wood pulp

a. the time between the last killing frost in the spring, and the first killing frost in the fall
b. wood that is ground into a thick liquid and used to make paper and paper products
c. trees that lose their leaves in the fall
d. cloth
e. the area where rivers fall from the Piedmont Plateau to the coastal plains
f. a whirling storm that forms over the ocean in tropical regions
g. a shallow place in the ocean where fish feed

Complete these activities.

2.8 The state with the largest land area in the Northeast is

_____ .

2.9 The state with the smallest land area in the Northeast is

_____ .

2.10 The state that is farthest south in the Northeastern region is

_____ .

2.11 Name the nine states that have an Atlantic coastline.

a. _____   f. _____

b. _____   g. _____

c. _____   h. _____

d. _____   i. _____

e. _____

2.12 Name the four Northeastern states that share a border with Canada.

a. _____   c. _____

b. _____   d. _____

Complete these activities.

2.13   Write the names of three Northeastern mountain ranges.

a. _____ , b. _____ , c. _____

2.14   Bays and estuaries make good harbors. Name three important harbors in the Northeast.

a. _____

b. _____

c. _____

2.15   Which two great lakes are located in the Northeast?

a. _____   b. _____

2.16   There is evidence that the Northeast was once covered with _____

_____ that scraped away the soil and dug _____ .

2.17   Climate is affected by the distance from the _____ ,

distance from a large body of _____ ,

and _____ .

2.18   _____ Falls is between Lake Erie and Lake Ontario.

2.19   Lake _____ is between Vermont and New York.

2.20   List five Northeastern rivers.

a. _____

b. _____

c. _____

d. _____

e. _____

Agriculture. Farmers tap the maple trees in spring for sap to make the famous Vermont maple syrup. Cranberries and potatoes grow in the lowlands, blueberries grow on the northern hills. Apples, grapes, peaches, and vegetables are grown along the Erie-Ontario Plain, the Atlantic Coastal Plain, and the valleys of the highlands. The Atlantic Coastal Plain supports many truck farms that grow tomatoes, corn, onions, spinach, cabbage, and lettuce. Large poultry farms are located in Delaware, Maryland, and New York. Dairies are located throughout the region.

Industry. Manufactured products of the Northeast include metal objects such as propellers, hard hats, needles, silverware, and brassware. Leather products manufactured are shoes and gloves. Wood pulp is used to make paper, much of which is used locally. This region has one of the biggest publishing industries in the world. **Textile** factories produce thread and cotton and woolen fabrics that are used in the clothing factories.

Early industrialists used the numerous waterfalls in the area to help produce energy to run their machines. Many large

HISTORY & GEOGRAPHY

703

703

LIFEPAC TEST

66 / 82

Name _____

Date _____

Score _____

HISTORY & GEOGRAPHY 703: LIFEPAC TEST

From the choices below, write the letter of the correct answer on the line (each answer, 2 points).

a. Northeast   b. Southern   c. Midwest   d. Western

1. Select the region where the Rocky Mountain rain shadow can be found. _____

2. Select the region where the Hudson and Mohawk Rivers can be found. _____

3. Select the region where the Piedmont Plateau can be found. _____

4. Select the region where Maine can be found. _____

5. Select the region where the Ozarks can be found. _____

6. Select the region where Arizona can be found. _____

7. Select the region where the Louisiana Purchase can be found. _____

8. Select the region where Lake Champlain can be found. _____

9. Select the region where Mt. McKinley can be found. _____

10. Select the region where Reconstruction took place following the Civil War. _____

11. Select the region where the American Industrial Revolution began. _____

12. Select the region that is known as the breadbasket of the United States. _____

13. Select the region where Lakes Superior, Michigan, and Huron can be found. _____

14. Select the region where Oklahoma can be found. _____

15. Select the region where the Great Plains are located. _____

16. Select the region where the Massachusetts Bay Colony was begun. _____

17. Select the region where Columbia, Snake, and Yukon Rivers are located. _____

18. Select the region where the Mississippi, Savannah, and Shenandoah Rivers are located. _____

19. Select the region where Illinois is located. _____

20. Select the region where Idaho can be found. _____

Write the letter of the correct answer on each line (each answer, 2 points).

21. The oldest mountains in our nation are _____ .
    a. the Rockies   c. the Appalachians
    b. the Sierra Nevadas

22. Many crops grow in the _____ .
    a. Intermountain region   c. coastal plains region
    b. Ozark Highlands region

23. Which of these states is a peninsula? _____
    a. Indiana   c. Oregon

    b. Michigan

24. The mechanical reaper invented by Cyrus McCormack helped the _____ .
    a. Midwest   c. West
    b. South

25. The first state was admitted to the Union in what year? _____

    a. 1807   c. 1787

    b. 1776

26. Henry Hudson claimed land in America for both England and what other
    nation? _____
    a. Spain   c. France
    b. Holland

27. Who was the president of the Confederate States of America? _____
    a. Jefferson Davis   c. Abraham Lincoln
    b. Robert E. Lee

28. The White, Catskill, and Blue Ridge Mountains are a part of what landform?
    _____

    a. Ozark Highlands   c. Appalachian Highlands
    b. Superior Uplands

29. Which European nation explored the Southwest? _____
    a. Spain   c. England
    b. France

30. In which of the following states is the growing season the longest? _____
    a. Montana   c. Hawaii
    b. Pennsylvania

Answer *true* **or** *false* (each answer, 1 point).

31. _____ Maine was one of the thirteen original states.

32. _____ Washington D.C. is in the northeast region.

33. _____ The United States has no active volcanoes.

34. _____ Glaciers have all disappeared from the United States.

35. _____ Much of the nation's wheat is grown on the Great Plains.

36. _____ The Volcanic Mountains landform includes Alaska and Oregon.

37. _____ The first Europeans to explore America were the Vikings of Norway

38. _____ California's population grew quickly after silver was discovered there in 1920.

39. _____ Pineapple and sugar cane grow well in the Hawaiian climate.

40. _____ Uranium is found in the mines of Pennsylvania.

Answer the following questions about your state (each question, 3 points)

41. Describe your state. What is your state bird, flower, tree, motto...?

_____

_____

_____

42. In what region of the United States is your state, and what are its natural land-forms?

_____

_____

_____

43. What are the most important crops and industries in your state?

_____

_____

_____

44. What is your state's largest city, and what is the capital?

_____

_____

3

manufacturing cities are located close to the rivers and falls in the region.

The Industrial Revolution in the United States began in the Northeast where the first factories were started. The very first factory was started by Samuel Slater in Pawtucket, Rhode Island in the year 1789. Slater brought the technology to use water power to spin thread from his native England. American inventor Eli Whitney furthered the American industrial advance when he designed a machine that made individual gun parts. This machine made all the parts in each gun exactly alike so that they could be interchanged. This invention was the beginning of mass production and led to an industrial boom in the Northeast. Because factories need many workers, the industrial cities of the Northeast are some of the largest cities in our country.

Answer *true* **or** *false.*

2.21 _____ Maple syrup is made from tree sap.

2.22 _____ The coastal plains support much agriculture.

2.23 _____ The Industrial Revolution began in the South.

2.24 _____ The Northeast has some of the largest cities.

2.25 _____ Samuel Slater designed a machine that made individual gun parts.

2.26 _____ Eli Whitney built a machine that used water power to spin thread.

Important historical events. The first European settlers in this region were people who came to the New World seeking religious freedom. The Pilgrims were actually Separatists seeking to leave what they considered to be the spiritually corrupt Church of England. They were imprisoned and driven out of England. They sailed from England across the Atlantic in the Mayflower and landed at Plymouth, Massachusetts, in December of 1620. During their first winter in the New World, many of the Pilgrims died. Eventually, however, they learned how to plant and hunt in their new home with help from some of the local Native American people. By fall the Pilgrims had plenty of food in Plymouth. The grateful Pilgrims invited the Indians to a feast lasting several days to thank God for His bounty. We remember that feast as Thanksgiving Day.

In the following years other colonists traveled to the northeastern area of the United States. Groups of Puritans, people who wanted to remain in the Church of England and purify it, settled and formed many communities as they also were driven out of England. The Massachusetts Bay Colony near Boston was one of the most famous of the Puritan communities.

The Revolutionary War, the War for Independence, was fought on the coast and in the highlands of the Northeast. The Boston Tea Party, the Boston Massacre, Paul Revere's ride, the signing of the Declaration of Independence, the battles of Valley Forge, Lexington, and Concord all occurred in the Northeast.

Complete these statements.

2.27 The _____ wanted to leave the Church of England while the _____ wanted to purify it.

2.28 The Massachusetts Bay Colony was settled by _____ , who were also driven out of England.

2.29 Much of the _____ War was fought on the coast and in the highlands of the Northeast.

Match these items.

2.30 _____ December, 1620   a. ship the Pilgrims sailed from England

2.31 _____ *Mayflower*   b. machine for picking fruit

2.32 _____ Pilgrims   c. looked for religious freedom

                                       d. Pilgrims landed at Plymouth

---

South

Much of the South was first explored and claimed by the Spanish. The first English settlement in the New World was established in this region in 1587 on Roanoke Island off the coast of North Carolina. The first English child born in America, Virginia Dare, was born here. However, the colony did not survive. The first permanent European settlements were founded here in St. Augustine, Florida, in 1565 by the Spanish and at Jamestown, Virginia, in 1607 by the English. The first African people were brought to Virginia in 1619. The system of slavery grew and flourished in the region until the Civil War.

The states considered to be Southern states are Alabama, Arkansas, Florida, Georgia, Kentucky, Louisiana, Mississippi, North Carolina, South Carolina, Tennessee, Virginia, and West Virginia.

Geography of the South. Geography in the South is varied. The natural landform regions are the Atlantic and Gulf coastal plains, the Appalachian Highlands, the Ozark Highlands, and the Interior plains and lowlands. More than half of the land area of the South lies in the Atlantic and Gulf coastal plains. Here the soil is light and sandy, good for farming. The coastal plains are nearly flat and in some places so low that they are covered with swamps and marshes. During the spring floods, the rivers that cross these plains deposit rich fertile soil eroded from the highlands.

2.33   Name the five Southern states that have an Atlantic coastline.

a. _____   d. _____

b. _____   e. _____

c. _____

2.34   Name the four Southern states that have a Gulf coastline.

a. _____   d. _____

b. _____   e. _____

The Appalachian Highlands of this region can be divided into four parts: the Piedmont Plateau, the Blue Ridge, the Appalachian ridges and valleys, and the Appalachian Plateau.

The Piedmont Plateau is a wide, flat area that is higher than the coastal plains but lower than the highlands to the west. The plateau has a rocky subsurface, and the rivers that cross over the plateau do not cut deep valleys into the land. When the rivers reach the edge of this rocky shelf they gouge deep valleys in the soft, sandy soil of the plain and form waterfalls. The Piedmont Plateau extends from central Alabama through Georgia, the Carolinas, Virginia, Maryland, Pennsylvania, and Delaware.

A number of cities were established at the waterfalls when pioneers were stopped from further travel by the rushing water. These cities are called **fall line** cities. Columbus, Georgia; Macon, Georgia; Augusta, Georgia; Columbia, South Carolina; Raleigh, North Carolina; Richmond, Virginia; Washington, D.C.; Baltimore, Maryland; and Philadelphia, Pennsylvania, are all fall line cities.

The slopes of the Blue Ridge Mountains and the Appalachian Ridges are steep. The area is heavily wooded; therefore, building roads and railroads in this area is difficult. The mountains and plateaus in the Ozarks are not so tall as those in the Appalachian Highlands. Blue Mountain and Magazine Mountain are the tallest peaks at twenty-eight hundred feet above sea level.

The Central Lowlands and Great Plain begin just west of the Appalachian Plateau area and cross Kentucky, Tennessee, and Northern Alabama. Two lowland areas in this plain are Bluegrass region in Kentucky and the Nashville Basin in Tennessee. Here the soil is more fertile than the other plains areas of the South.

A particular feature of the South is the network of broad rivers that stretch throughout its lands. Settlers used these waterways for travel and for the transportation of goods throughout the South. The Ohio River at the northern edge of the region, the Mississippi (the largest river in the United States), the Alabama, the Tennessee, the Savannah, and the Shenandoah rivers are important to the region.

Write the correct letter and answer on the line.

2.35   The Bluegrass region of Kentucky is in the _____ of the South.

    a. lowland   b. upland   c. highland

Complete these activities.

2.36 Name five fall line cities.

a. _____   d. _____

b. _____   e. _____

c. _____

2.37 Circle the items that are true of the Piedmont Plateau.

It is a mountainous area.
It is a wide, flat area.
It has a rocky subsurface.
Waterfalls form at the downriver edge.
It covers the coast of Florida and Georgia.

2.38 Name four important rivers of the South.

a. _____   c. _____

b. _____   d. _____

2.39 More than half of the land in the South lies in the _____

and _____ coastal plains.

Climate. The climate of the South is very different from that of the Northeastern states. Here the winters are mild and the summers are warm. The only places that receive much snow are the highest mountains.

The South receives more rain than any other region in the United States. Many parts of the South get more than forty inches of rainfall during the year. This moisture contributes to the high humidity of the region and plays a part in the thunderstorms and **hurricanes** that are characteristic summer weather in the South.

 Study the rainfall chart and answer the questions.

Average Monthly Precipitation in Richmond, Virginia

inches	Jan.	Feb.	Mar.	Apr.	May	June	July	Aug.	Sept.	Oct.	Nov.	Dec.	centimeters
5													12.7
4													10.2
3													7.6
2													5.1
1													2.5

2.40   Which month was the driest month?_____

2.41   Which month had the most rain?_____

Write the correct letter and answer on the line.

2.42   Rainfall makes most of the South very _____.

     a. dry   b. humid   c. warm

Photo by Carlyle Calvin

Natural resources. Timber is one of the South's natural resources. Turpentine, rosin, wood pulp, paper, lumber, and furniture are produced from the trees in this region. The hills of West Virginia, Kentucky, Tennessee, the Carolinas, and Arkansas yield coal, iron ore, sulfur, salt, clay, granite, and marble. Petroleum and natural gas are also found. The fishermen bring in bass, shrimp, oysters, sea trout, red snapper, and crabs.

Agriculture. The farmers of the South produce apples, citrus fruit, cotton, peaches, peanuts, vegetables, rice, soybeans, and sugar cane. Georgia grows more peaches than any other state in the region. Florida raises winter vegetables and most of the citrus fruit in the region. Farms in Florida also produce potatoes and strawberries. Louisiana farmers grow sugar cane and rice.

Industry. After the Civil War, Northern mill owners moved their textile mills to this region. Textiles are still an important product of Southern factories. Processed foods (such as peanut butter and cooking oil) and chemicals are another important industry. Products manufactured in the South are easily transported to other parts of the nation and other countries for distribution because of the transportation resources of fine ports and harbors on the Atlantic and Gulf coasts. Many of the large cities in the South are port cities.

Important historical events. The South was the location of the most devastating war ever fought on American soil, the Civil War. It devastated the South even as it divided our nation. The key points of the division were over a high tariff imposed on the Southern states, the issue of slavery, and whether or not states could leave the Union. The Southern states seceded from the Union in the 1861 and began a war to make the separation permanent.

The South formed a new nation, called the Confederate States of America, and chose Jefferson Davis as their president. The South quickly fielded an army and took over the forts of the U.S. army in the South. The rest of the country, under the leadership of President Abraham Lincoln, fought to retain the Union and, eventually, to end slavery forever.

Many courageous men fought in the Civil War. General (later President) Ulysses S. Grant was on the Union side. General Robert E. Lee and General Stonewall Jackson are two famous men who fought on the Confederate side.

In the end, the superior supplies of both men and material from the Union won the war. General Lee surrendered to General Grant at Appomattox Courthouse, Virginia, on April 9, 1865 after more than 600,000 men had died, many of disease. The Civil War ended slavery in the Southern states. The North had ended slavery well before the war by passing laws against it in all of the Northern states.

Five days after the South's surrender, President Lincoln was shot by John Wilkes Booth, an actor who was angry because the

South lost the war. That assassination cost the South its last hope for an easy peace.

The United States Congress, unhindered by Mr. Lincoln's morals, wanted to punish the Southern states before they could be readmitted to the Union. This period was called Reconstruction. Congress wanted the Reconstruction governments to help the new African American citizens, but these governments were not in power for long. By 1877 Reconstruction was over, and all the Southern states had been readmitted to the Union.

Tenant farming developed at the end of the Civil War when most plantation owners no longer had slaves and did not have the money to hire workers. The plantation owners agreed that the tenant farmer would live and work on a small plot of land during the year. At the end of the year, the tenant farmer(also called a sharecropper) would give the owner a share of the harvest or crop. Tenant farming methods were often poor and resulted in soil depletion and erosion. Southern farmland suffered from these effects for many years and kept the farmers of the South poor.

Write the correct letter and answer on the line.

2.43   Another name for tenant farming is _____ .
         a. sharecropping   b. renting   c. owning

2.44   Where did General Lee surrender at the end of the Civil War?

         _____
         a. Richmond, Virginia   b. Washington, D.C.   c. Appomattox Court-house

2.45   President Lincoln was assassinated by whom? _____
         a. Robert E. Lee   b. John Wilkes Booth
         c. Stonewall Jackson   d. Lee Harvey Oswald

2.46   The Civil War lasted over what time period? _____
         a. 1861-1865   b. 1880-1893   c. 1843-1862

Review the material in this section in preparation for the Self Test. This Self Test will check your mastery of this particular section as well as your knowledge of the previous section.

SELF TEST 2

Match these items and related terms (each answer, 2 points).

2.01 _____ scoured land

2.02 _____ Great Lake

2.03 _____ fall line city

2.04 _____ trees

2.05 _____ citrus

2.06 _____ manufacturing

2.07 _____ 1861-1865

2.08 _____ Thanksgiving

2.09 _____ coastal plains

2.010 _____ agriculture

a. industry
b. Florida
c. glaciers
d. Pilgrims
e. Richmond, Virginia
f. Erie
g. the South
h. New York, New York
i. wood pulp
j. Civil War
k. farms

Write *true* **or** *false* (each answer, 1 point).

2.011 _____ The Northeast is wetter than the South.

2.012 _____ Cranberries grow well in the Northeast.

2.013 _____ Glaciers retreated, leaving lakes behind.

2.014 _____ Deciduous trees stay green all the year.

2.015 _____ Connecticut, Maine, Rhode Island, New Hampshire, and Vermont are some of the New England States.

2.016 _____ Jefferson Davis was the president of the Confederate States of America.

2.017 _____ Settlers used rivers for travel and exploration.

2.018 _____ The Kentucky Bluegrass region is highland.

2.019 _____ The coastal plains are fertile.

2.020 _____ Cotton grows well in the Northeast.

Write the letter of the correct answer on the line (each answer, 2 points).

2.021 A state is a _____ region.
   a. landform   b. natural   c. political

2.022 Maple syrup is an agricultural product from _____ .
   a. Vermont   b. Delaware   c. Alabama

2.023 The Appalachian Mountains are the _____ in the U.S.
   a. oldest   b. tallest   c. youngest

2.024 The landform region that is *best* for farming is the _____ .
   a. Appalachian Highland   b. Ozark Plateau   c. coastal plains

2.025 Early New England factories used _____ to run their machines.
   a. coal   b. gas   c. waterfalls

Complete these statements (each answer, 3 points).

2.026 The first people who came to America for religious freedom were

_____ .

2.027 The three nations that explored most of the United States were
   a._____ , b._____ , and c._____ .

2.028 The two oceans that make the coasts of the United States are
   a._____ and b._____ .

2.029 Hawaii and Alaska were admitted to the Union in _____ .

Answer these questions (each answer, 5 points).

2.030 Climate is affected by the distance from the a. _____ ,
   distance from a large body of b. _____ , and the
   c. _____ .

2.031 _____ formed along the downriver side of the Piedmont and were used for manufacturing power.

2.032 _____ was the period of time when Congress tried to punish the South for the Civil War.

2.033 In the United States, the Industrial Revolution began in the _____ region.

2.034 After the Civil War, the agriculture of the South developed around _____ because plantation owners did not have cash to pay workers.

---

77 / 96		Score _____
		Teacher check _____
		Initial Date

III. PHYSICAL AND CULTURAL REGIONS OF THE MIDWEST AND THE WEST

The regions you will study in this section are the Midwest and West. These lands became part of the United States at a later time than did the Northeast and South. Alaska and Hawaii were only admitted to the Union in 1959. The western states cover the largest share of the land in the United States.

SECTION OBJECTIVES

Review these objectives. When you have completed this section, you should be able to:

1. Use maps and globes as a source of information about the Midwestern and Western United States.

2. Describe the landforms, climate, and early history of the Midwestern and Western United States.

3. Describe the landforms and climate in your own state.

4. Explain the effect of climate and landforms on occupations, agriculture, and industry in your own states and in the four regions of the of the United States.

VOCABULARY

Study these words to enhance your learning success in this section.

blizzard (bliz´ urd). A severe snowstorm with high winds.
levee (lev´ ē). A bank built next to a river to prevent it from flooding.
mission (mish´ un). A building where missionaries live and work.
rain shadow (rān shad´ ō). Land on the inland or leeward side of mountains.
tornado (tôr nā´ dō). A severe wind storm with a funnel-shaped cloud.

28

MIDWEST

Part of the Midwest region has a humid climate that supports many trees. This section is called the Central Lowland or the Interior Lowland. The other section is dryer grassland that rises toward the west to a higher elevation than the lowlands. This section is called the Great Plains. It extends through western North Dakota, South Dakota, Nebraska, Kansas, Oklahoma, and Texas. The states in the Central Lowland are Illinois, Indiana, Iowa, Michigan, Minnesota, Missouri, Ohio, and Wisconsin.

Geography of the Midwest. More than three-fourths of the Midwest is in the Central Lowlands and the Great Plains, but three other natural landform regions are included in the Midwest. The Appalachian Plateau is in Ohio; the edges of the Ozark Highlands are in Missouri and Oklahoma; and the Superior Upland is in Michigan, Minnesota, and Wisconsin.

The Superior Upland is hilly with a few low mountains. Dense forests and thousands of lakes are found here. Lake Superior, the largest of the five Great Lakes, is in this region.

Three great rivers flow through the Midwest: the Ohio, the Missouri, and the Mississippi. With their tributaries they form a great drainage basin in the center of the United States. Texas has the Rio Grande at its Mexican border.

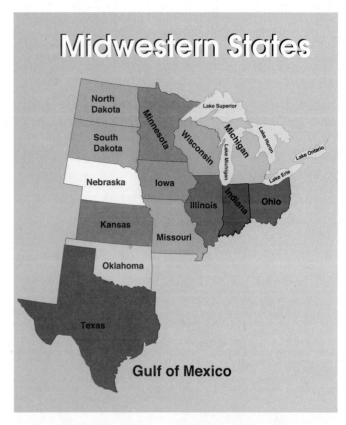

Midwestern States

Photo by Eric Wunrow

In the Great Plains the land is much drier. Prairie grass grows here. Farmers must depend on irrigation to grow crops. Sometimes this area receives less than twenty inches of rainfall in a year. The land is mostly flat but in some places steep hills rise above the rest of the land. The Black Hills of South Dakota and the Badlands are two areas of highland in the plains. The Black Hills are covered with pine trees. From a distance they make the hills look black. Mount Rushmore is a popular tourist attraction in the Black Hills.

The other highland area in the Great Plains is the Badlands. This area was once a high plateau, but over the years the rain and wind have carried away soil and rock, eroding deep gullies and leaving high, craggy rock formations pointing toward the sky. Erosion in the Badlands left hills and valleys of sand, gravel, and clay layered with limestone and sandstone. However, no soil remains that will support plant life.

Climate. In the Midwest the summers are much warmer and the winters much colder than they are in other areas in the same latitude. One reason for this difference is the distance from the ocean. Another important reason is the wind.

In the summer, winds come from the south. They are closer to the equator and, therefore, are warmer. In the winter the winds blow from the north across Canada before they get to the lowlands and plains. There are no high mountains in this area to stop or divert the wind. This climate that has very warm summers and very cold winters is called a continental climate.

Photo by Carlyle Calvin

In the summer the winds that blow from the Gulf of Mexico also bring water-laden clouds. The eastern part of this region has many thunderstorms in the summer. The winds also bring **tornados** and **blizzards** to this region. Each year in the spring and early summer, tornados destroy property and crops worth many millions of dollars.

One reason why the western part of this region receives so little rain is because it lies in the **rain shadow** of the Rockies. As westerly winds blow across the Pacific Ocean, they pick up moisture. When these winds rise above the high peaks, they cool and lose this moisture as rain or snow in the high mountains. When the winds move down the eastern ranges, they are dry. The winds warm as they move down and take up moisture from the land, but they rarely drop this moisture back to the ground.

In the spring the rain and melting snow from the mountains swell the rushing rivers of the area. Severe flooding has occurred in the past; however, dams and **levees** now control the rivers so that fewer floods damage homes and crops.

In the northern part of the Midwest, the growing season is between three and five months long. In a few places it is less than three months long. In the southern part the growing season is five to seven months long with a few places having a growing season of seven to nine months.

⭐ **Complete these activities.**

3.1   The name of the state that has two separate parts is _____.

3.2   The name of the Great Lake that is farthest north is _____.

3.3   The only Great Lake that is totally within the borders of the United States is _____.

3.4   Name the states that have a Great Lakes shoreline. _____

_____

_____

Complete the vocabulary crossword.

3.5

ACROSS
1. A severe snowstorm with high winds.
2. A building where missionaries live and work.
3. A severe wind storm with a funnel-shaped cloud.

DOWN
1. A bank built next to a river to prevent it from flooding.
2. Land on the inland or leeward side of mountains.

Write the correct answer on each line.

3.6 Two differences between the Central Lowlands and the Great Plains in the Midwest are the _____ and the _____

a. elevation   c. hemisphere
b. latitude   d. rainfall

Write the correct letter and answer on the line.

3.7 A climate that has warm summers and cold winters is called a _____ climate.

a. varied   b. continental   c. severe

Complete these statements.

3.8 The western region of the Midwest is very dry because it is in the _____ of the _____ Mountains.

3.9 In the winter the winds of the Midwest blow from the north across _____ .

3.10 Name the three rivers of the Midwest.

a. _____

c. _____

b. _____

3.11 _____ by wind and rain left no soil for plant life in the Badlands.

3.12 The eastern Midwest is a windy area where _____ in the spring and summer destroy crops and property.

Natural resources. One of the most valuable resources of the Midwest is fertile soil. Other resources are timber, fur-bearing wild life, iron ore, coal, gold, sand, gravel, and stone. Copper, lead, and zinc are also mined in this region. Fishermen catch herring, pike, perch, and whitefish in the lakes. Oil fields and natural gas are abundant in some areas of the Midwest.

Photo by Eric Wunrow

Agriculture. The three most important agricultural areas in this region are the "corn belt" in Ohio, Indiana, Illinois, Iowa, Nebraska, South Dakota, Minnesota, Missouri, and Kansas; the "wheat belt" in North Dakota, Nebraska, Kansas, Oklahoma, Colorado, Montana, and South Dakota; the "hay and dairy belt" in Minnesota, Wisconsin, Michigan, Illinois, and Indiana. Other products grown in this region are soybeans, cotton, apples, cherries, straw-berries, blueberries, and vegetables. Large areas of land in the dry western part of this region are irrigated or used for grazing herds of cattle or sheep instead of farming. Texas has range land for cattle, but with irrigation it also produces fruit and vegetables and a large crop of cotton.

Industry. Availability of raw materials and the ease of transportation on the Great Lakes route or down the Mississippi have led the north central part of the Midwest to develop a number of important industries. Mills in Cleveland, Ohio; Gary, Indiana; Chicago, Illinois; and Detroit, Michigan produce steel for the cars and machinery manufactured in nearby factories.

Food processing plants, meat packing plants, textiles, printing, and publishing are the other large industries in this area. In the southern section of the Midwest are many large oil refineries.

When the railroad extended into the Midwest in the 1800s, ranchers began to drive their herds of cattle across the open range to Abilene, Kansas, along the Chisholm Trail. Other cowboys drove long-horns from Texas to Dodge City, Kansas, or to Kansas City, Missouri. Meat and bread could be processed and transported from these points in the Midwest to all the United States.

Match the following natural resources with the occupations they promote.

3.13	_____	fertile soil	a.	winter tourists
3.14	_____	lakes, rivers, oceans	b.	mining
3.15	_____	petroleum	c.	farming
3.16	_____	timber	d.	summer tourists
3.17	_____	snowy mountains	e.	printing and publishing
3.18	_____	iron ore	f.	fishing
3.19	_____	sandy beaches	g.	refining
3.20	_____	scenic views		

Complete these activities.

3.21   What are the three "belts" of agriculture in the Midwest?

a. _____

b. _____

c. _____

3.22   The most valuable resource of the Midwest is the _____ soil.

3.23   The western part of the Midwest is often used for _____ herds of animals

3.24   When the railroad reached the Midwest in the 1800s, ranchers drove cattle to Abilene, Kansas to meet the trains along the _____ Trail.

- -

Important historical events. The first steps toward the settlement of the Midwest came when Daniel Boone blazed a trail through the Cumberland Gap in 1775. Thousands of pioneers followed him into the wilderness west of the Appalachians. After the Revolutionary War many people traveled down the Ohio River by flatboat to reach the frontier with its promise of abundant land and a better life. In 1785 and 1787 Congress passed the Northwest Ordinance that set a plan for admitting new states into the nation as the territories grew in population.

As more settlers came to the West and the frontier was pushed back, the United States had the opportunity to buy the vast area of land owned by France that included the Mississippi River and the Port of New Orleans. President Jefferson made the Louisiana Purchase in 1803. Then Jefferson sent Lewis and Clark, two explorers, to explore, map, and survey the land.

Still more settlers came, walking or in covered wagons. Settlers wanted the land for themselves. They killed many of the Indians and forced the rest onto reservations.

Oklahoma was set aside as Indian Territory. The five civilized tribes, the Cherokee, Creek, Chickasaw, Choctaw, and Seminole, were forced to leave their homes in the east and travel to this area between 1820 and 1846. A treaty was signed and the Indians were to own this land forever. However, during the Civil War the agents of these tribes supported the Confederacy, and the United States ruled that the Indians no longer had the right to own this land. Oklahoma was open to settlers.

The settlers cultivated the fertile land and made large grain producing farms. In 1831 Cyrus McCormick built a mechanical reaper that greatly affected the Midwest. The reaper provided a way for acres and acres of wheat to be harvested with only a few workers. The Midwest became the "breadbasket" of the nation.

▶ ▶ ▶ **Complete these statements.**

3.25　Name two people who explored part of the Midwest for President Jefferson.

　　　a._____ and b._____

3.26　Many Indians were forced from their homeland when the settlers moved west. Name the territory that the United States set aside for the Indians.

　　　_____

3.27　Daniel Boone blazed the trail through the _____ Gap.

3.28　The invention of the mechanical reaper by _____ transformed wheat production in the Midwest.

WEST

The states in the West are Alaska, Arizona, California, Colorado, Hawaii, Idaho, Montana, Nevada, New Mexico, Oregon, Utah, Washington, and Wyoming. Much of the land is mountainous. Hawaii has an active volcano. Alaska has glaciers.

Geography of the West. The landform regions of the Western states are the Great Plains, the Rocky Mountains, the Intermountain Region, the Pacific Coast Mountain and Valley Region, the Volcanic Rock Region of the Hawaiian Islands and the mountains, valleys, and plains of the Alaskan Peninsula and islands.

The Rocky Mountains are both the highest and the longest mountain range in the continental United States. The only mountains higher than these in the North American continent are in Alaska in the Alaskan range.

In the Rockies, snow covers the tops of some of the highest peaks all year. The

Volcanic crater – Mt. Kiluea, Hawaii

Rockies have large evergreen forests on the lower slopes. Because building roads for transporting people and goods is so difficult, very few people live in these mountains.

The Intermountain Region has many high plateaus. Some places have low

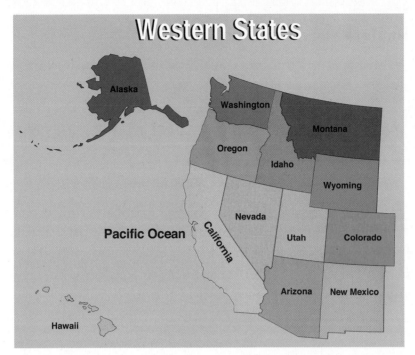

Western States

mountains and valleys. In some places the plateaus have been cut by rivers flowing across the land. For many years the Colorado River has eroded a vast canyon into the Colorado Plateau. This canyon, in Arizona, is called the Grand Canyon and it is more than a mile deep in some places.

Between the mountains are some partly flat, bowl-shaped areas called basins. In the central part of this Intermountain Region is the Great Basin. The water that flows into the basin area from the mountain streams and the rain does not reach the ocean. In this area the water collects in small ponds or lakes. Salt and other minerals that were in the water are left on the land when the water evaporates. When the water does not evaporate but instead forms a lake, the lake is very salty. The great Salt Lake in Utah is one of these lakes.

The Cascade Range in the north, the Olympic Range in the northwest, the Sierra Nevada Range in the south, and the Coast Range in the west are the mountains of California, Oregon, and Washington.

Mount Whitney in California is the highest point in the continental United States at 14,494 feet(4,418 m).

Mount McKinley in Alaska is the highest point on the North American continent at 20,329 feet (6,194 m). Death Valley, California is the lowest point in the continental United States reaching down to 282 feet (86 m) below sea level.

The important rivers in this region are the Columbia River in Washington, the Snake River in Idaho and Washington, the Willamette River in Oregon, the Sacramento River in California, the Yukon River in Alaska, and the Colorado River in Utah and Arizona.

Complete these activities.

3.29   The states that share a border with Mexico are_____

_____.

3.30   Write the names of the four states that meet at a single point.

a._____ b._____ c._____ d._____

3.31   Name the western states that border Canada.

a._____ b._____ c._____ d._____

Complete these statements.

3.32　　The land feature that was cut into the Colorado Plateau by the rushing Colorado River is called the

_____ .

3.33　　Name the three mountain ranges near the Pacific coast.

a. _____

b. _____

c. _____

3.34　　The name of the highest mountain in the continental United States is Mount _____ .

3.35　　The central area of the Intermountain Region where water in streams is trapped and evaporates is called the

_____ .

Complete this activity.

3.36　　List four important rivers of the Western region.

a. _____

b. _____

c. _____

d. _____

Climate. The climate in the Intermountain area of this region is very dry. Less than twenty inches of rain falls in this area in a year. The mountains of northern California, Oregon, and Washington receive much more precipitation. The tropical islands of Hawaii receive heavy rainfall on the windward sides of the land. In the northern part of the West, the winters are cold and snowy. In Alaska the temperature often drops to 30° below zero. In the southern part of the West and along the coast, the winters are mild. In the summer the southern part of the region is very hot and the northern part is mild. One area in the West is different. This area is in the rain shadow of the Rockies; here the summers are hot and the winters are severely cold.

Some areas where the snow is on the ground all year have almost no growing season. In other places like the Arctic Slope in Alaska, the growing season is less than two months long. In the southern latitudes the growing season is much longer. The growing season in southern California is eight months long, and in most of Hawaii it is twelve months long.

 **Study the temperature chart.**

Average Monthly Temperatures
Pt. Barrow, Alaska

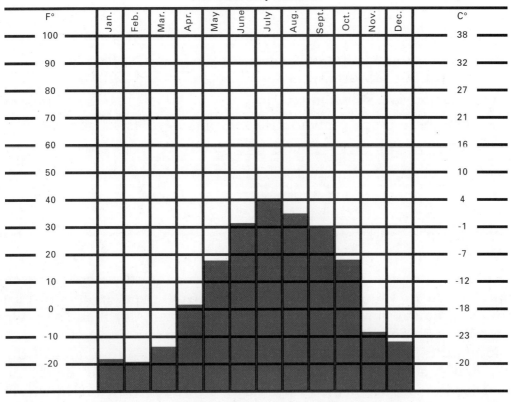

3.37 Referring to the chart above, what month was the coldest in Alaska?

_____

3.38 Referring to the chart above, what month was the warmest in Alaska?

_____

Natural resources. Timber for wood pulp and lumber is abundant in the forests of Oregon, Washington, Idaho, Alaska, and California. The redwood trees in California and Oregon are some of the tallest living trees in the world. Under the fertile soil are deposits of soda ash, iron ore, petroleum, natural gas, gold, copper, zinc, silver, lead, tungsten, and uranium. Fishermen haul in catches of salmon, halibut, cod, mackerel, trout, shad, and bass. The Pacific fleets bring albacore and bonita tuna and swordfish into the Western ports.

Agriculture. The range of climate, soil, and water availability produces good conditions for the growth of many crops. Fruit, vegetables, cotton, nuts, and grain are all grown in this area. Washington grows more apples than any other state. Hawaii has its fields of pineapple, sugar cane, and coffee. The California grape vineyards and orange groves are world famous. In many of the dry areas of the West, farmers must use dry farming methods or rely on irrigation for watering their crops. The farming areas of Northern California, Oregon, and Washington are three areas in this region that receive adequate rainfall.

Complete these activities.

3.39 Name three important metals that are mined in the West.

a. _____

b. _____

c. _____

3.40 California and Oregon's _____ trees are some of the tallest in the world.

3.41 Washington grows more _____ than any other state.

3.42 List three crops grown in Hawaii that were listed above.

a. _____

b. _____

c. _____

Industry. Sawmills in the Northwest are part of the timber industry that produces lumber and wood pulp for paper. Other factories produce metal products; build cars, ships, airplanes and missiles; and make clothing. Oil refineries, iron and steel plants, and food processing plants are big industries in this region.

Oil refinery

Important historical events. Spanish explorers were the first Europeans in the Southwest (southern part of the far West). After Coronado's explorations in 1540, an expedition led by Juán Rodriguez Cabrillo sailed the length of the California coastline looking for riches and a water route through North America. The very dry climate and lack of water made this area difficult to settle.

An Englishman named Sir Francis Drake sailed into a quiet bay near San Francisco when he sailed around the world from 1577 to 1580. He claimed this area for England. However, no one ever followed up on the claim. Settlers did not come to the area for many years after the first explorations. Santa Fe, New Mexico, the oldest capital city in our country, was not founded until 1609. Portola did not lead the first group of settlers to the San Francisco area until 1769.

When the Spanish and Mexican settlers came to the West, they built many **missions**. The San Diego mission was built in 1769. In 1776, the same year the colonists were signing the Declaration of Independence on the east coast, Spanish missionaries founded San Juan Capistrano on the west coast. The Spanish built twenty-one missions along El Camino Real, "The King's Highway" along California's coast. The Spanish settlers also built

Photo by Carlyle Calvin

villages and forts. In 1781 a group of settlers started the village of *Nuestra Senora la Reina de los Angeles*. This settlement grew into the largest city in the Western region, Los Angeles, California.

When Mexico gained control over this Spanish land, many ranches were built. Most of the people raised cattle. When ships from the United States sailed into the harbors, the Californians traded hides and other raw products for goods from New England factories.

Complete these activities.

3.43 Write the name of the little village that grew into the biggest city on the west coast. _____

3.44 The first Europeans to explore the Southwest were the

_____ .

3.45 The Spanish built a string of _____ along California's coast in the late 18th century.

3.46 Most of the settlers in the Southwest raised _____ on their ranches.

3.47 The Englishman _____ once claimed part of California for England on his voyage around the world.

Other early explorers in this region were the Russian trappers who moved down the coast of Alaska and Canada looking for fur-bearing animals. Americans Zebulon Pike, John C. Fremont, and the Native American woman Sacajawea, who guided Lewis and Clark, found routes overland through the Northwest to the Pacific.

Many people moved to the West in the early 1800s. They traveled across the Rockies in long wagon trains to California and Oregon. Oregon became part of the United States when Great Britain and America signed a treaty in 1846 settling their dispute over the area. California became part of the United States after the Mexican War (1846-48) when Mexico ceded all the land north of the Rio Grande to America.

Gold was discovered in California in 1848, and thousands of people came to California hoping to strike it rich in the gold fields. They came in wagon trains or sailed around Cape Horn of South America. Some tried a shorter route, cutting their way across the Isthmus of Panama.

In 1862 Congress passed the Homestead Act, which gave 160 acres of free land to the families that moved to the west. Then, in 1869, railroad workers met at Promontory, Utah, completing the first railroad line all the way across the nation. The railroad made it possible for more people to move west quickly. More people move to the region every year. The West still continues to grow today as people moved out of the decaying industrial cities of the North and East.

3.48   People rushed to California after _____ was discovered there in 1848.

3.49   Oregon became a part of the United States after the border dispute with _____ was settled by treaty in 1846.

3.50   The _____ Act gave 160 acres of free land to families that moved west.

Before you take this last Self Test, you may want to do one or more of these self checks.

1.   _____   Read the objectives. See if you can do them.

2.   _____   Restudy the material related to any objectives that you cannot do.

3.   _____   Use the SQ3R study procedure to review the material:

a. **S**can the sections.
b. **Q**uestion yourself.
c. **R**ead to answer your questions.
d. **R**ecite the answers to yourself.
e. **R**eview areas you did not understand.

4.   _____   Review all vocabulary, activities, and Self Tests, writing a correct answer for every wrong answer.

SELF TEST 3

Answer *true* **or** *false* (each answer, 1 point).

3.01   _____   Most of the states in the Great Plains get more rain than the states in the Northeast because they are in the rain shadow of the Rockies.

3.02   _____   California was first settled by the Spanish.

3.03   _____   Oregon became a part of the United States as a result of the Mexican War (1846-1848).

3.04   _____   The Great Salt Lake is salty because it is so close to the ocean.

3.05   _____   Alaska has the highest peak in the United States.

3.06   _____   The oldest capital city in the United States is St. Augustine, Florida.

3.07   _____   Washington D.C. is in the Southern region of our country.

3.08   _____   The Midwest is called the "breadbasket" of the nation.

3.09   _____   The Louisiana Purchase was made by President Washington.

3.010   _____   The Appalachians are in the Western United States.

Write the letter for the correct answer on each line (each answer, 2 points).

3.011   The kind of farming that developed in the South at the end of the Civil War
was _____.
a. dry farming   b. tenant farming   c. irrigated farming

3.012   Which of these explorers claimed land in the New World for two
countries?_____
a. Champlain   b. Coronado   c. Hudson

3.013   The Grand Banks are an important _____ region.
a. farming   b. fishing   c. mining

3.014   The region that is just east of the fall line cities is the _____.
a. coastal plain   b. Piedmont Plateau   c. Intermountain region

3.015   The Grand Canyon is in _____.
a. Utah   b. Arizona   c. Colorado

3.016   How long is the growing season in Hawaii? _____.
a. 3 months   b. 5 months   c. 12 months

3.017   The mechanical reaper invented by McCormick helped the _____.
a. Midwest   b. West   c. South

3.018   Which of these lakes is a Great Lake? _____
a. Champlain   b. Superior   c. Salt Lake

3.019   Cowboys drove cattle herds to market in the _____.
a. West   b. Midwest   c. South

3.020   This river is a tributary of the Mississippi: _____.
a. Columbia   b. Rio Grande   c. Ohio

Complete these statements (each answer, 3 points).

3.021   The American Southwest was first explored by the _____ .

3.022   The _____ Act encouraged settlement of the west by
giving new families 160 acres of free land.

3.023   The geographical feature that led to the development of factories in the
Northeast was _____ .

3.024   _____ was originally set aside as Indian territory.

3.025   The two oceans that make up the coast of the United States are
the _____ Ocean and the _____ Ocean

41

Match each region with its description. (each answer, 2 points).

3.026 _____ Appalachian Highlands

3.027 _____ Atlantic and Gulf coastal plain

3.028 _____ Ozark Highlands

3.029 _____ Central Lowlands and Great Plains

3.030 _____ Superior Uplands

3.031 _____ Rocky Mountain Region

3.032 _____ Intermountain region

3.033 _____ Pacific Coast Mountains and Valleys

3.034 _____ Volcanic Mountains

a. Hawaiian Islands

b. includes White, Adirondack, and Catskill Mountains

c. includes Alaska and America's tallest mountain

d. waterfalls mark the edge of the Piedmont Plateau

e. the Great Basin and Great Salt Lake

f. small range of low mountains and hills in south central U.S.

g. highest and longest range of mountains in the U.S.

h. dominates center of the U.S.

i. heavily wooded lake area at western edge of the Great Lakes

53 / 66		Score _____ Teacher check _____ Initial Date

Before taking the LIFEPAC Test, you may want to do one or more of these self checks.

1. _____ Read the objectives. See if you can do them.

2. _____ Restudy the material related to any objectives that you cannot do.

3. _____ Use the SQ3R study procedure to review the material.

4. _____ Review activities, Self Tests, and LIFEPAC vocabulary words.

5. _____ Restudy areas of weakness indicated by the last Self Test.